JUL 2009

W9-CJD-143

The new Solar System

Venus

Robin Birch

CHELSEA CLUBHOUSE

An Imprint of Chelsea House Publishers

Chelsea Clubhouse
An imprint of Chelsea House Publishers
132 West 31st Street
New York, NY 10001

Chelsea Clubhouse books are available at special discounts when purchased in bulk quantities for businesses, associations, institutions, or sales promotions. Please call our Special Sales Department in New York at (212) 967-8800 or (800) 322-8755.

You can find Chelsea Clubhouse on the World Wide Web at: http://www.chelseahouse.com

First published in 2004 by
MACMILLAN EDUCATION AUSTRALIA PTY LTD
15–19 Claremont Street, South Yarra, 3141

Visit our Web site at www.macmillan.com.au or go directly to www.macmillanlibrary.com.au

Associated companies and representatives throughout the world.

Copyright © Robin Birch 2004

Library of Congress Cataloging-in-Publication Data

Birch, Robin.
   Venus / Robin Birch. – 2nd ed.
   p. cm. — (The new solar system)
   Includes index.
   ISBN 978-1-60413-209-0
   1. Venus (Planet)—Juvenile literature. I. Title.
   QB621.B57 2008
   523.42—dc22

                              2007051544

Edited by Anna Fern
Text and cover design by Cristina Neri, Canary Graphic Design
Photo research by Legend Images
Illustrations by Melissa Webb, Noisypics

Printed in the United States of America

Acknowledgements
The author and publisher are grateful to the following for permission to reproduce copyright material:

Cover photograph of Venus courtesy of Photodisc.

Art Archive, p. 5 (top); D. Parer & E. Parer-Cook/Auscape, p. 15; Australian Picture Library/Corbis, p. 23 (top); Digital Vision, pp. 5 (bottom), 26; Calvin J. Hamilton, pp. 7, 11, 21; Walter Myers/www.arcadiastreet.com, p. 10; NASA/JPL, pp. 16 (right), 18, 19, 20, 28 (both); NASA/JPL/Caltech, p. 17; NASA/NSSDC, pp. 24, 25; NASA/US Geological Survey, p. 27; Photodisc, p. 29 (top); Photolibrary.com, p. 29 (bottom); Photolibrary.com/NASA/SPL, p. 12; Photolibrary.com/SPL, pp. 4 (bottom right), 6, 13, 14, 16 (left), 22 (both), 23 (bottom).

Background and border images, including view of Venus, courtesy of Photodisc.

While every care has been taken to trace and acknowledge copyright, the publisher offers their apologies for any accidental infringement where copyright has proved untraceable. Where the attempt has been unsuccessful, the publisher welcomes information that would redress the situation.

Please note
At the time of printing, the Internet addresses appearing in this book were correct. Owing to the dynamic nature of the Internet, however, we cannot guarantee that all these addresses will remain correct.

Contents

Glossary words

When you see a word printed in bold, **like this**, you can look up its meaning in the glossary on page 31.

Discovering Venus

Venus is a **planet** that looks like a very bright **star**. Venus is the third brightest object in the sky, after the Sun and the Moon. Venus is always fairly close to the Sun in the sky, and can sometimes be seen in the western sky, not long after sunset. Venus can sometimes be seen in the eastern sky, too, for a while before sunrise. Venus is often called the "morning star" when it appears in the morning or the "evening star" when it appears after sunset.

◄ This is the symbol for Venus.

Venus

The word "planet" means "wanderer." Stars always make the same pattern in the sky. Planets change their location in the sky, compared to the stars around them. This is why they were called "wanderers."

▲ Venus in the evening sky

◀ The Roman
goddess Venus

Venus is named after Venus, the Roman goddess of love and beauty. The planet Venus was probably given this name because it is very bright and beautiful.

Venus looks like a bright object through a **telescope**, but no details can be seen. More than 20 spacecraft have visited Venus to find out more about it. In 1962, the first **space probe**, called *Mariner 2*, visited Venus. The space probe *Magellan* visited Venus in 1991 and 1992. It sent back the best information so far about the surface of Venus.

▲ The planet Venus

5

The Second Planet

The planet Venus **revolves** around the Sun, along with seven other planets and many other bodies. The Sun, planets, and other bodies together are called the solar system. Venus is the second planet from the Sun.

There are eight planets in the solar system. Mercury, Venus, Earth, and Mars are made of rock. They are the smallest planets, and are closest to the Sun. Jupiter, Saturn, Uranus, and Neptune are made mainly of **gas** and liquid. They are the largest planets, and are farthest from the Sun.

The solar system also has dwarf planets. The first three bodies to be called dwarf planets were Ceres, Pluto, and Eris. Ceres is an asteroid. Pluto and Eris are known as **trans-Neptunian objects**.

A planet is a body that:

- orbits the Sun
- is nearly round in shape
- has cleared the area around its orbit (its **gravity** is strong enough)

A dwarf planet is a body that:

- orbits the Sun
- is nearly round in shape
- has not cleared the area around its orbit
- is not a **moon**

▲ The solar system

There are also many small solar system bodies in the solar system. These include asteroids, comets, trans-Neptunian objects, and other small bodies which have not been called dwarf planets.

Asteroids are made of rock. Most of them, including dwarf planet Ceres, orbit the Sun in a path called the asteroid belt. The asteroid belt lies between the orbits of Mars and Jupiter. Comets are made mainly of ice and rock. When their orbits bring them close to the Sun, comets grow a tail. Trans-Neptunian objects are icy, and orbit the Sun farther out on average than Neptune.

▶ The eight planets are Mercury, Venus, Earth, Mars, Jupiter, Saturn, Uranus, and Neptune.

The solar system is about 4,600 million years old.

Planet	Average distance from Sun	
Mercury	35,960,000 miles	(57,910,000 kilometers)
Venus	67,190,000 miles	(108,200,000 kilometers)
Earth	92,900,000 miles	(149,600,000 kilometers)
Mars	141,550,000 miles	(227,940,000 kilometers)
Jupiter	483,340,000 miles	(778,330,000 kilometers)
Saturn	887,660,000 miles	(1,429,400,000 kilometers)
Uranus	1,782,880,000 miles	(2,870,990,000 kilometers)
Neptune	2,796,000,000 miles	(4,504,000,000 kilometers)

The name "solar system" comes from the word "Sol," the Latin name for the Sun.

On Venus

As it travels around the Sun, the rocky planet Venus spins on its **axis**.

Rotation and Revolution

Venus **rotates** very slowly on its axis once every 243 Earth days—the slowest rotation of all the planets. Venus does not have seasons, because it rotates in an almost upright position.

Compared to other planets, Venus rotates backward. A person on Venus would see the Sun rise in the west and set in the east. On Earth, the Sun rises in the east and sets in the west.

Venus orbits the Sun every 225 Earth days, which is the length of one year on Venus. Venus has only two sunrises per year. Its day, from sunrise to sunrise, is 117 Earth days long, due to its slow backward rotation and its long year. The Sun's gravity keeps Venus revolving around it.

As they orbit the Sun, Venus and Earth sometimes come closer together than at other times. At the point when Venus and Earth come closest together, the same side of Venus always faces Earth.

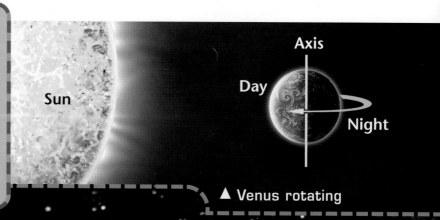

Sun

Axis

Day

Night

▲ Venus rotating

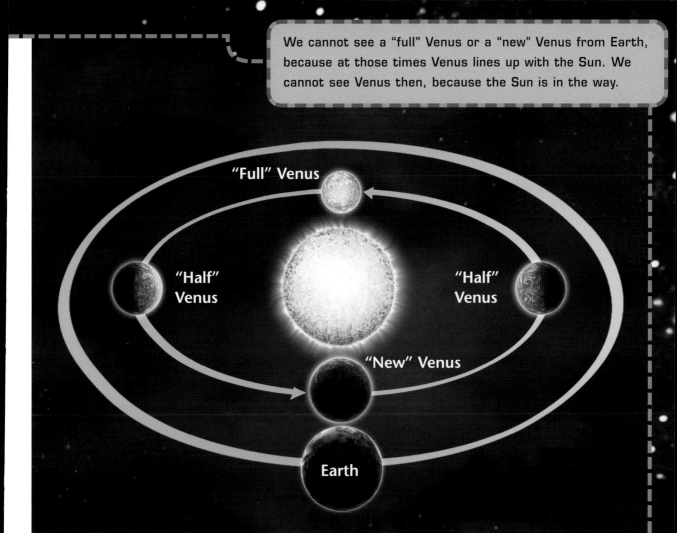

We cannot see a "full" Venus or a "new" Venus from Earth, because at those times Venus lines up with the Sun. We cannot see Venus then, because the Sun is in the way.

"Full" Venus

"Half" Venus

"Half" Venus

"New" Venus

Earth

▲ The phases of Venus

Phases

Venus appears round when seen without a telescope. This is because Venus is extremely bright. When viewed through a telescope from Earth, Venus appears to change its shape, in the same way that the Moon does. These changes in shape are called "phases."

We see the phases of Venus because Venus is closer to the Sun than we are on Earth. As Venus orbits the Sun, the sunlight shines on Venus from different directions. For example, the Sun may shine on the left or right side of Venus, as seen from here on Earth. Then we would see a "half" Venus through a telescope.

Size and Structure

Venus is 7,517 miles (12,104 kilometers) in **diameter**, which is a similar size to Earth. Venus also has a similar **mass** and **density** to Earth, and could almost be called Earth's sister planet.

Astronomers have worked out what Venus is probably like on the inside by looking at measurements of gravity and **magnetism** taken by space probes. Astronomers think Venus is similar to Earth on the inside. It probably has a **core** made of iron about 1,900 miles (3,000 kilometers) in diameter. The core may be solid, or it may be hot and **molten**.

▲ Compare the size of Venus (right) to Earth (left).

Venus does not have a **magnetic field**. Usually, if a planet has an iron core, it is surrounded by a magnetic field. Earth has an iron core and a strong magnetic field. Venus probably does not have a magnetic field because it spins very slowly.

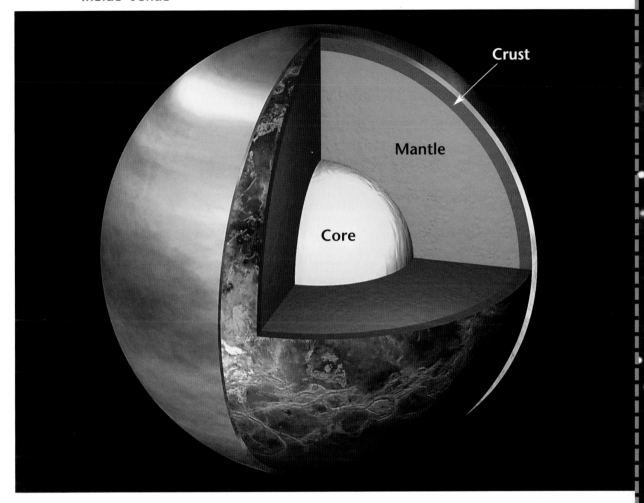

Venus has a **mantle** around the core. The mantle takes up most of the planet. It is made of hot, molten rock.

Venus has a strong, thick crust as its outside layer. The crust is all in one hard piece and is mostly between 16 and 25 miles (25 and 40 kilometers) thick. It is made of hard, reddish-brown rock. In many places there are cracks, which formed when parts of the crust pushed on each other. In the places with cracks, **lava** can escape from the mantle below the crust, making **volcanoes** and other features.

11

Atmosphere

Venus has a thick **atmosphere**, made mostly of carbon dioxide gas. There is almost no water in the atmosphere. The atmosphere has a very high **pressure**—90 times the pressure of Earth's atmosphere. Space probes which have landed on Venus have only lasted a few hours before they have been crushed by the atmosphere.

Venus has very thick clouds in its atmosphere which cover the whole planet. We cannot see through the clouds to the surface. Venus looks very bright to us because the clouds reflect a lot of sunlight.

Winds in the highest clouds blow at 220 miles per hour (350 kilometers per hour)—faster than a hurricane on Earth. Winds at the surface of Venus are slow.

The light at the surface of Venus is a dim orange color. This is because clouds stop most of the sunlight from getting through.

▶ Clouds cover the planet Venus.

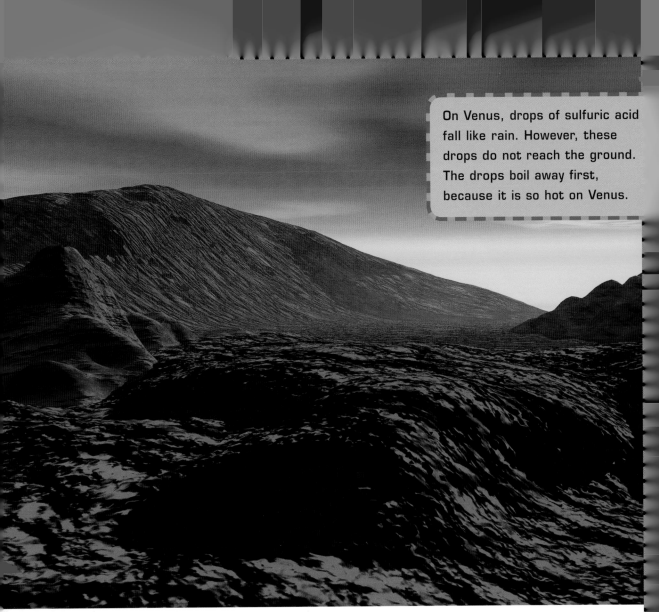

On Venus, drops of sulfuric acid fall like rain. However, these drops do not reach the ground. The drops boil away first, because it is so hot on Venus.

▲ An artist's impression of the surface of Venus

Temperature

The clouds of Venus are mostly high up in the atmosphere. They are made of drops of sulfuric acid, a strong, burning substance. (Clouds on Earth are made of drops of water.) The thick clouds on Venus keep heat from the Sun trapped below them, like a blanket. This is why Venus is very hot. At 900 degrees Fahrenheit (480 degrees Celsius), Venus is the hottest planet.

Surface Features

Venus has reddish-brown rocky ground. There is no water on the ground. Gentle winds blow at ground level. The wind is just strong enough to blow sand along to make sand dunes.

Most of Venus is covered with smooth, gently sloping plains. The plains are formed from lava which has flowed out of openings in the crust. The lava has cooled to form a fairly smooth surface. The plains are called lowlands.

There are also some high, mountainous areas, called the highlands. They take up about one-tenth of Venus.

▼ An artist's impression of lava flows on Venus

▲ Lava flowing around a volcano on Earth has formed this plain. This also happened on Venus.

The oldest land on Venus is only about 800 million years old. (A lot of land on Mercury, and on Mars and Earth's Moon is more than 4,000 million years old.) This is because there has been so much lava flowing over the surface of Venus.

Volcanoes

Venus has many volcanoes. There are more than 1,000 volcanoes which are more than 12 miles (20 kilometers) in diameter. Venus has many more smaller volcanoes, which are not known to be active. Astronomers think some volcanoes may possibly be active.

The volcanoes on Venus are mostly shield volcanoes. Shield volcanoes have thin lava which spreads out over a wide area. This makes them wide and low rather than tall and narrow. It also makes wide plains around the volcanoes, where the lava has spread out.

Domes

Venus has volcanic domes on its surface, ranging from less than 6 miles (10 kilometers) across to 60 miles (100 kilometers) across. They can be up to 1 mile (2 kilometers) high. Domes are circular in shape, have a steep outside edge and a fairly flat top. They may have formed from very thick, sticky lava that came out of a hole in the ground at the center of each one.

The lava probably welled up inside the domes, which made the surface stretch.

Ticks

Venus has a type of volcano that astronomers have nicknamed "ticks," because they look like a tick (a small creature related to a spider). The volcanoes have a fairly flat top with ridges and valleys that spread outwards, so they look like legs. Lava has spilled out on one side, which looks like a head. So far, 50 of these tick-shaped volcanoes have been found on Venus.

▼ A "tick"

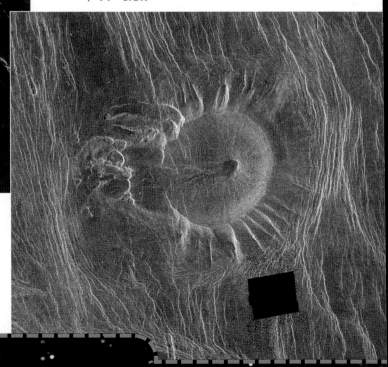

 ▲ The pancake domes are a group of seven overlapping volcanic domes. They are each about 16 miles (25 kilometers) in diameter and up to 2,500 feet (750 meters) high.

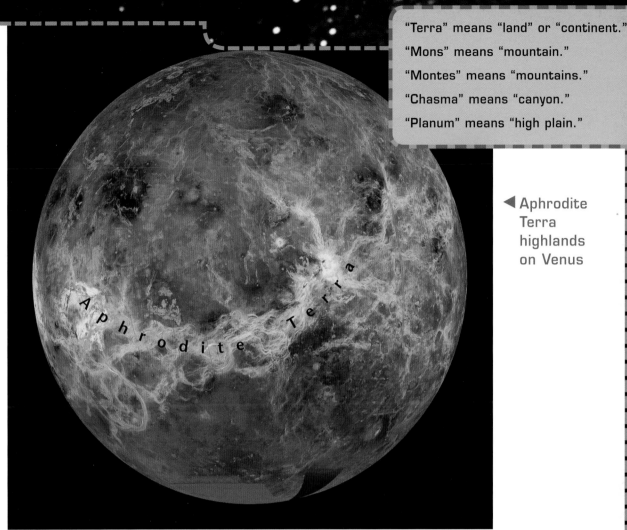

◀ Aphrodite Terra highlands on Venus

Aphrodite Terra

Aphrodite Terra is the largest highland area on Venus. It is about the same size as South America and runs nearly halfway around the **equator** of Venus.

Aphrodite Terra has many large volcanoes on it, such as the 5-mile-high (8-kilometer) volcano Maat Mons. There are long, deep valleys at the eastern end of Aphrodite Terra. One of them, Diana Chasma, is 2.5 miles (4 kilometers) deep.

Images of Venus show the higher parts of Aphrodite Terra to be rather bright. These bright areas possibly have the substance commonly called "fool's gold" in the rocks on the surface.

Ishtar Terra

Ishtar Terra is the smaller of the two main highland areas of Venus. Ishtar Terra is about the same size as Australia. It is near the north **pole** of Venus.

Ishtar Terra is a large **basin** which has filled with lava. The lava has cooled and set hard. Towards the middle of Ishtar Terra is a large, high area called Lakshmi Planum. Lakshmi Planum is a high plain, about 1.5 to 2.5 miles (2.5 to 4 kilometers) high. Lakshmi Planum has mountains around it, which are the highest on Venus. These include the enormous Maxwell Montes, the tallest mountains of all. They are up to 7 miles (12 kilometers) high.

Aphrodite and Ishtar were goddesses of love.

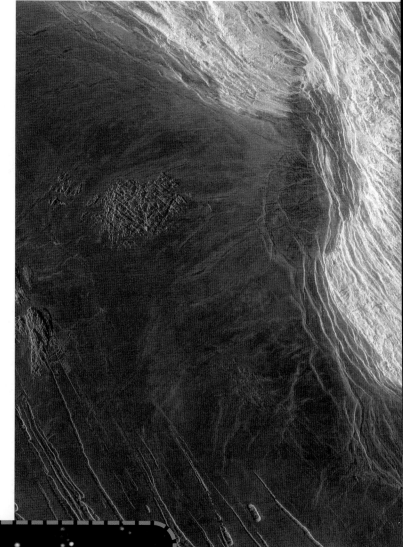

▶ The Maxwell Montes mountains on Venus

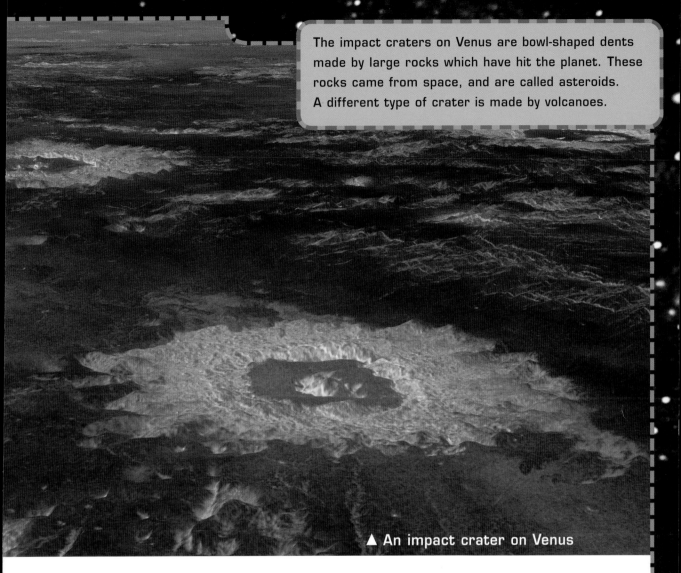

The impact craters on Venus are bowl-shaped dents made by large rocks which have hit the planet. These rocks came from space, and are called asteroids. A different type of crater is made by volcanoes.

▲ An impact crater on Venus

Craters

Venus has many impact **craters** on its surface, but not nearly as many as the planet Mercury. Venus has been hit by just as many asteroids as Mercury, but when a rock flies through Venus's thick atmosphere, it burns up. Only very big rocks reach the ground to make craters, which is why most craters on Venus are large, more than 1 mile (2 kilometers) in diameter. Mercury has hardly any atmosphere, so all rocks that hit Mercury reach the ground, making more craters on Mercury than on Venus.

19

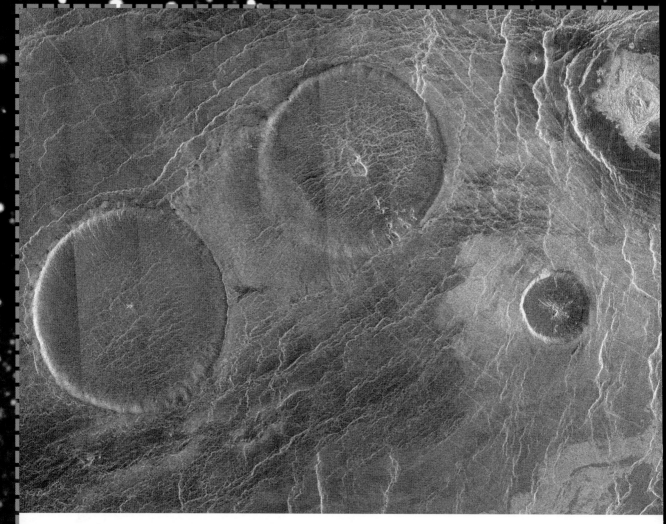

▲ A group of impact craters on Venus

Venus has several groups of impact craters on its surface. This is because some large asteroids broke into pieces just before reaching the ground and each piece made a crater.

Old craters on Venus have been covered up by lava flowing from volcanoes. Most of the craters on Venus and the other planets were made 4,000 million years ago, when the solar system was young. A lot of lava has flowed over the surface of Venus since then, so Venus is fairly smooth. The oldest land on Venus is only about 800 million years old.

Calderas

Venus has giant, basin-shaped hollows called calderas. The calderas are shaped either like circles or like ovals and are more than 60 miles (100 kilometers) in diameter. Usually calderas on planets are only several miles in diameter.

Calderas are made when lava has flowed into an underground space. The lava suddenly leaves the space because it has been blown out, or because it has sunk back into the ground. The roof of the space then collapses, making the hollow caldera.

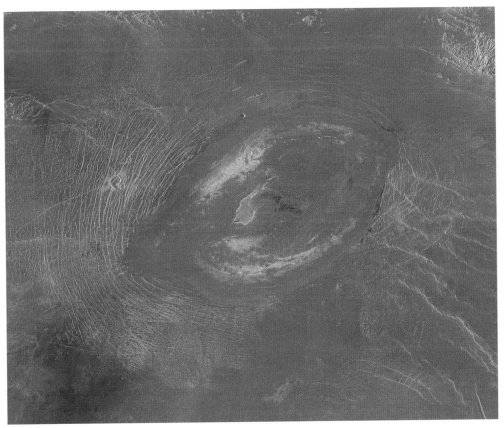

▲ This caldera, called Sacajawea Patera, is about 75 miles (120 kilometers) wide, 130 miles (215 kilometers) long, and .6 to 1.2 miles (1 to 2 kilometers) deep. It is located in Ishtar Terra and is circled by cliffs.

"Corona" means "crown."
"Coronae" is the word for
more than one corona.

Coronae

Coronae are found only on Venus, not on other planets. A corona is a circular or oval mound, with a hollow area around it. Coronae are probably caused by the ground being pushed up by lava, then dropping down again. They can be hundreds of miles across. They have cliffs forming circles around them as well as lines spreading outwards from them. These lines are cracks in the surface filled with lava that has become solid.

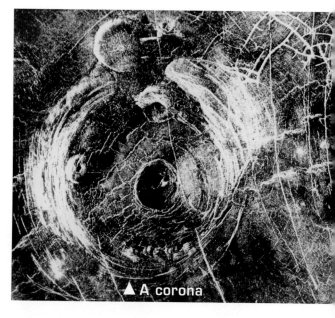

▲ A corona

Arachnoids

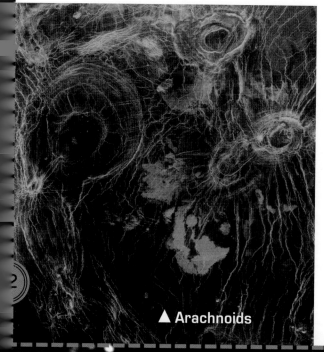

▲ Arachnoids

Arachnoids are also found only on Venus. They are similar to coronae, but are usually smaller, about 30 to 140 miles (50 to 230 kilometers) across. They have rings around them, and lines spreading outwards. The word "arachnoid" means "like a spider." Astronomers thought arachnoids looked like spiders with long legs.

Channels

Venus has long
channels winding
across its plains. These
channels are hundreds
to thousands of miles
long and usually have
no branching. They
are filled with lava
that has set hard.

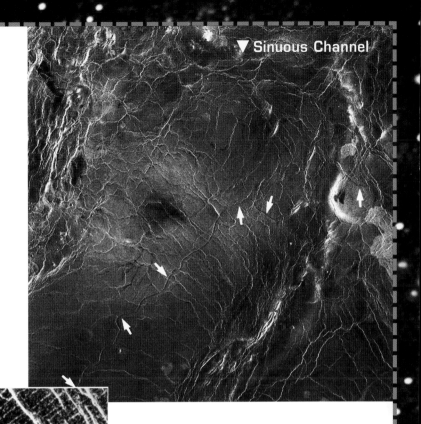

▼ Sinuous Channel

Lines

An area of Venus has two
groups of lines on it which
cross each other, making
a criss-cross pattern. The
fainter lines are about
half a mile (1 kilometer)
apart. The brighter lines
are not so evenly spaced.
The lines are probably
cracks in the ground.

◄ Pattern of lines on Venus

23

Exploring Venus

Astronomers on Earth have tried to study Venus using telescopes, but Venus has very thick clouds which hide the surface of the planet. Only the cloud tops can be seen, with telescopes. The only way to study the surface of Venus is to send space probes there.

More than 20 space probes have visited Venus. The first space probe to go there was *Mariner 2* in 1962. The probe's instruments measured heat and microwaves coming from Venus, so that astronomers could figure out the temperature on the planet.

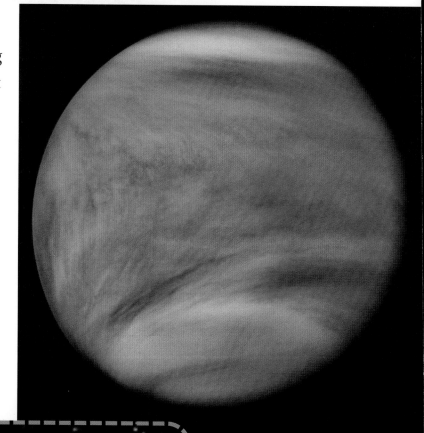

▶ Cloud tops on Venus

24

▲ An artist's impression of the *Pioneer 12* probe orbiting Venus

Space Probes

The space probe *Venera 7* landed on Venus in 1970. It sent information back to Earth for 23 minutes. *Venera 9* landed on Venus in 1975. It sent the first pictures of the ground on Venus back to Earth. In 1978 *Pioneer 12* and *Pioneer 13* arrived at Venus. *Pioneer 12* made a map of Venus using radar, and *Pioneer 13* found that the bottom 20 miles (30 kilometers) of the atmosphere of Venus was clear.

The best information we have about Venus comes from the *Magellan* probe, which reached Venus in 1990. Another probe, *Venus Express*, reached Venus in 2006. It discovered a huge windstorm at Venus's south pole.

Magellan Space Probe

The space probe *Magellan* visited Venus from 1990 to 1994. *Magellan* was launched into space on board the space shuttle *Atlantis* in 1989. *Magellan* then separated from *Atlantis*. It took *Magellan* 15 months to reach Venus.

Magellan orbited around Venus many times and made maps of 98 percent of the surface. *Magellan* used radar to detect the features on Venus, such as mountains, plains, and craters. It could not take photographs of the ground on Venus because clouds were in the way. *Magellan* also made maps of the gravity of Venus. In 1994, *Magellan* dropped into the atmosphere of Venus and was crushed by the thick atmosphere.

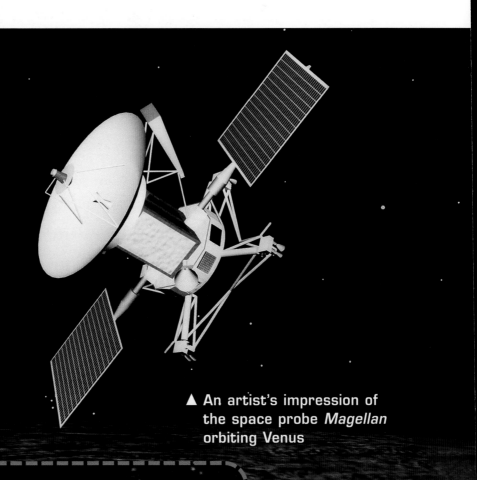

▲ An artist's impression of the space probe *Magellan* orbiting Venus

The pictures made from the *Magellan* information have been colored, to show mountains and valleys. The sky is black in the *Magellan* pictures, but the sky on Venus is really full of thick orange-yellow clouds.

▲ This picture of Venus was made from information gathered by *Magellan* using radar.

The features on Venus were mapped by a radar instrument on board *Magellan*. **Radio waves** which were sent down to Venus bounced off the surface and were collected by the radar instrument. The different shapes on Venus bounced the radio waves back in different ways.

The information gathered was beamed back to Earth, using radio waves. Astronomers put this information together, to make pictures. The pictures made in this way look like photographs, but they are not.

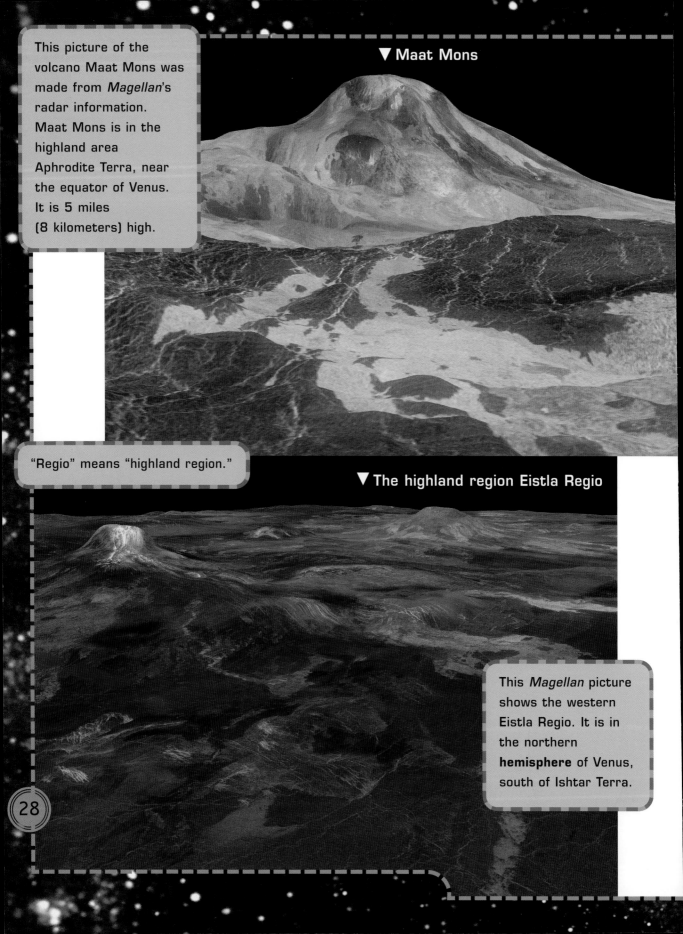

This picture of the volcano Maat Mons was made from *Magellan*'s radar information. Maat Mons is in the highland area Aphrodite Terra, near the equator of Venus. It is 5 miles (8 kilometers) high.

▼ Maat Mons

"Regio" means "highland region."

▼ The highland region Eistla Regio

This *Magellan* picture shows the western Eistla Regio. It is in the northern **hemisphere** of Venus, south of Ishtar Terra.

Questions about Venus

There is still a lot to learn about Venus. One day, astronomers hope to find out the answers to questions such as these:

- Venus and Earth are similar in make up, and they formed at the same time. Why, then, has Venus turned out to be so different from Earth?

- Why doesn't Venus's crust move as Earth's does? Is it because Venus is much hotter than Earth?

- Why is the atmosphere of Venus so thick? Why does it have so much carbon dioxide in it?

- How big is the core of Venus? Is it solid or liquid?

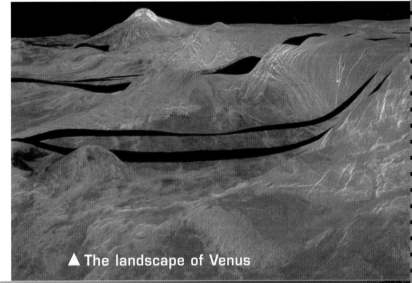

▲ The landscape of Venus

▶ Compare the Earth's landscape to that of Venus

Venus Fact Summary

Distance from Sun (average)	67,190,000 miles (108,200,000 kilometers)
Diameter (at equator)	7,517 miles (12,104 kilometers)
Mass	0.82 times Earth's mass
Density	5.24 times the density of water
Gravity	0.91 times Earth's gravity
Temperature (surface)	900 degrees Fahrenheit (480 degrees Celsius)
Rotation on axis	243 Earth days
Revolution	225 Earth days
Number of moons	0

Web Sites

www.jpl.nasa.gov/magellan/
Magellan mission to Venus, 1989–1994

www.nineplanets.org/
The eight planets—a tour of the solar system

www.enchantedlearning.com
Enchanted Learning Web site—click on "Astronomy"

stardate.org
Stargazing with the University of Texas McDonald Observatory

pds.jpl.nasa.gov/planets/welcome.htm
Images from NASA's planetary exploration program

Glossary

astronomers people who study stars, planets, and other bodies in space

atmosphere a layer of gas around a large body in space

axis an imaginary line through the middle of an object, from top to bottom

basin a very large, bowl-shaped hollow

core the center, or middle part of a solar system body

craters bowl-shaped hollows in the ground

density a measure of how heavy something is for its size

diameter the distance across

equator an imaginary line around the middle of a globe

gas a substance in which the particles are far apart, not solid or liquid

gravity a force which pulls one body towards another body

hemisphere half of a globe

lava hot liquid rock

magnetic field an area where magnetism occurs

magnetism a force which a magnet has, to attract other similar objects

mantle the middle layer, underneath the crust

mass a measure of how much substance is in something

molten melted into a liquid

moon natural body which circles around a planet or other body

orbit *noun* the path a body takes when it moves around another body; *verb* to travel on a path around another body

planet a large, round body which circles the Sun, and does not share its orbit with other bodies (except its moons)

pole the top or bottom of a globe

pressure a force pushing on something

radio waves invisible rays which can carry information

revolve travel around another body

rotates spins

space probe an unmanned spacecraft

star a huge ball of glowing gas in space

telescope an instrument for making objects look bigger and more detailed

trans-Neptunian objects small solar system bodies which orbit the Sun farther out than Neptune, on average

volcanoes holes in the ground through which lava flows

Index